COMMIT!

HOW TO TURN YOUR VISION
OF CHANGE INTO A REALITY

COMMIT!

HOW TO TURN YOUR VISION OF CHANGE INTO A REALITY

A LEADERSHIP HANDBOOK

BY
MARION STODDART WITH WORKOF1000.ORG

MARION STODDART
THE WORK OF 1000
DOCUMENTARY PROJECT

COMMIT!
HOW TO TURN YOUR VISION
OF CHANGE INTO A REALITY

A Leadership Handbook
By Marion Stoddart with Workof1000.org
Published by Work of 1000
info@workof1000.org | **workof1000.org**

For information on bulk purchases or educational use,
please contact 978.433.5697 or info@workof1000.org

ISBN 978-0-578-04249-7

LEADERSHIP | SOCIAL CHANGE | ENVIRONMENTAL CONSERVATION & PROTECTION | RIVERS | WOMEN CONSERVATIONISTS

"You don't have to be someone special or someone super bright or super anything. You can just be an ordinary person who first has a vision of what you would like to have happen who then makes a commitment to that vision."

–MARION STODDART

PREFACE

In the turbulent decade of the 1960s, Americans faced monumental changes. The nation's political and social creeds were shifting; the grassroots were igniting, questioning everything from the war in Vietnam to social injustice to the degradation of our natural environment. Internationalism, feminism, the Civil Rights Movement, the War on Poverty, the right to human health and wellness—dramatic changes were unfolding. It was during this era that the phrase *"Think Global, Act Local"* was coined.

In 1962 the Nashua River meandered through the urban and rural communities of north central Massachusetts toward its final destination, the Merrimack River in New Hampshire. Once pristine and teeming with wildlife, the Nashua had been declared *"biologically dead."* Cleaning the Nashua seemed hopeless. As the Nashua reached this lowest point in its life, housewife and mother Marion Stoddart considered the direction her own life was taking. *"Why am I here on this earth?"* she wondered, *"What is it I'm supposed to be doing?"*

Living a mile from the Nashua's polluted waters, Marion, not knowing how she'd do it, committed herself to the greatest purpose she could imagine accomplishing during her lifetime— restoring the river. During years of tenacious advocacy, Marion convinced community leaders, stakeholders, and citizens that change was possible. They joined the fight and under Marion's leadership, the river was rescued. Federal and State laws were passed, including the Massachusetts Clean Water Act.

Marion was heralded as an environmental hero. She was awarded the United Nations Environmental Programme's Global 500 Award, profiled in *National Geographic*, and featured in a widely-read children's book. She is also the subject of a documentary film, *Marion Stoddart: The Work of 1000*.

This book is designed to help you achieve the same successes as Marion Stoddart. If you are a student, an activist, or a person wanting to make change in your community, this Leadership Handbook will give you the practical tools to turn your vision for change into a reality.

—SUSAN EDWARDS, *Producer, Work of 1000*

"I'm grateful for Marion's commitment to her vision of a clean Nashua River. Economic revitalization depends heavily on taking full responsibility for, and making full use of, the natural environment of one's community. As I work toward the economic revitalization of Fitchburg, I am inspired daily by Marion's determination and her approach to leadership detailed in this handbook."

–HONORABLE LISA WONG
Mayor of Fitchburg, Massachusetts

HOW TO USE THIS BOOK

This book has all the questions, and you have all the answers. Write them down! Putting pen to paper is absolutely essential for refining, honing, and sharpening your vision.

Be specific. When you're answering a huge question like *"What is your vision?"* make sure to include the details—the names and the places—that will help you think more clearly. And remember, the answers you write down here are for you. You can always refine them later when enlisting others in your vision.

Get Inspired. If Marion Stoddart— just one person— can change her small part of the world, imagine if every person were empowered to do *"the work of 1000."* Go to **www.workof1000.org** if you're feeling overwhelmed and need a jump-start of inspiration.

"Making change is never easy, but it is particularly difficult in hard times. But as this book shows, we can each make a difference and, imagine the impact if we work together. Working together to improve our rivers, our communities and the environment can have some wonderful side effects including bringing together diverse groups and introducing girls and boys (and adults) to science in exciting new ways."

–PATRICIA B. CAMPBELL, PH.D.
  Researcher in Science and Math Education Equity. Campbell-Kibler Associates, Inc.

MARION'S STORY

By 1962 the Nashua River had become an open sewer. The river was biologically dead. Its horrible reek could be smelled a mile away, and its eerie colors assaulted the senses. The Nashua was choked by waste and starved of oxygen—one of the 10 most polluted rivers in America.

Living only a mile from the Nashua's polluted waters, Marion Stoddart was inspired by something she heard in a radio program: that with vision and commitment, *"one person can do the work of 1000."* Even before a clear plan had formed in her mind, Marion committed herself to restoring the river to its earlier health.

Many believed Marion to be out of her mind; the river was well beyond hope and impossible to revive. But Marion knew to her core that with hard work and perseverance the river could be saved.

The Nashua had long been a dumping ground for people, factories, and communities along the river. There were no laws that prohibited discharging municipal or industrial waste into waterways. Paper, plastic, and textile companies dumped their wastes directly into rivers. Cities discharged raw sewage. Some municipalities located their dumps next to the river for easy garbage disposal. The river was so grossly polluted that no one thought it would make any difference to add more pollutants. The river became thick with sludge and multi-colored dyes.

5

For generations the public and scientists believed that pollutants were simply *"flushed"* away by the river. However, by the early 1960s, like other rivers around the country, the Nashua was no longer *"flushing"* waste away. Sick and dying, it wasn't even clear the river could be saved.

START WITH A DREAM OR A VISION OF WHAT YOU WANT

Marion began her campaign full of hope, thoroughly committed to her vision of a restored and beautiful Nashua River. She saw a river teeming with fish and wildlife, bordered and protected by a corridor of woods, fields, and trails. A river that people would have access to and learn to love, appreciate, and care for. A river that would sustain life and revitalize its cities.

COMMIT TO THAT VISION

Marion's husband Hugh quipped that *"Marion has a lover and her lover is the river."* Every surface in her home was so crowded with papers, her daughter's friend asked, *"Is your mother the mailman?"* Her children heard taunts at school about their *"crazy"* mother and Marion *"the Queen of the Nashua,"* not a compliment.

There were even dire threats. She had to tell herself that her work on the river was too important to give up. She was truly committed to her vision of a restored Nashua River.

EDUCATE YOURSELF ON THE ISSUES

Marion was determined that the Nashua River prevail against both industrial and municipal pollution, so she spent a great deal of her time learning all that she could about land and water resources, laws, and agencies.

IDENTIFY COMMUNITY LEADERS AND STAKEHOLDERS— ENLIST THEM IN YOUR VISION

Well-informed and resolute, she set out to contact every stakeholder in the Nashua River basin to enlist them in her vision for the river. She sought out leaders in business, government, and local communities. It was not easy work; no one wanted to associate with a challenge that seemed impossible. But Marion knew that with perseverance she could assemble a diverse group of thousands joining together to demand a clean river.

Another reason Marion was successful in her campaign to restore the Nashua was that she did not demonize industry. Instead, she sought to enlist them in the cause as well.

SURROUND YOURSELF WITH POSITIVE THINKING PEOPLE

With tireless determination and resilience, Marion gave tennis lessons to raise money, collected signatures on petitions, and knocked on doors. She made a commitment to be optimistic and surround herself with positive thinking people. She knew that naysayers to her vision would drain her energy.

EDUCATE OTHERS & BUILD RELATIONSHIPS

One of the most important relationships Marion built was with Fitchburg Mayor Bill Flynn. Flynn had been trying to lure a business owner to Fitchburg, but encountered some unexpected resistance. The condition of the Nashua, the executive said, demonstrated how little self-respect the city had. He would never relocate his business to a community with a river that vile. It was a wake-up call.

Collaborating with Marion on the campaign to clean up the river, Flynn—then only 25 years old—began championing the cleanup of the river by getting the City of Fitchburg behind the effort and helping to insure that State and Federal agencies paid their fair share of the cost.

Timing was right for public perceptions of the environment to change. Stewardship, human health concerns, and a desire for recreation began to replace the idea of the river as simply a facilitator of industry, a town dump, or an open sewer.

SEE "CHALLENGES" AS OPPORTUNITIES, NOT PROBLEMS. SEE "NO" AS AN EXCITING CHALLENGE

Marion began her fight as a Groton housewife in the early 1960s. But she didn't seem to be aware of her gender in her advocacy work. At a meeting, several years into her campaign, Marion recalls looking around the table and noticing another woman present. Suddenly, she was self-conscious about being a woman! Although aware that she was taking an atypical stance for a 1960s housewife, Marion rarely experienced moments like she did at this meeting.

Marion's work has often been praised as a triumph for feminism. But she was rarely conscious of her gender and the barriers she broke for gender equality was a fortunate by-product of her passion for the river. Marion did not acknowledge her limitations as a woman in this decade, and therefore was able to overcome oppressive stereotypes.

BE RECEPTIVE AND OPEN TO OPPORTUNITIES FROM UNEXPECTED PLACES AND PEOPLE.

Marion stuck to her ultimate goal. Her ability to persuade others to get involved resulted in collaboration with the military. Fort Devens, a nearby military installation, was located along more than 8 miles of the Nashua River. Fort Devens' Commanding Officer, Colonel John H. Cushman, heard about Marion's efforts to clean up the Nashua and offered to help. Over the years, Fort Devens provided office space and professional military staff to help prepare an environmental plan to protect land along the river and in the watershed. A collaboration with the military, the U.S. Department of Labor, the newly created EPA, and riverside communities resulted in the employment of over 400 teenagers and young adults in need of work experience. The youth helped with the river cleanup and trail building. Fort Devens provided thirteen Green Berets to oversee the work and thirteen Army dump trucks.

ASK FOR WHAT YOU WANT, NOT WHAT YOU'RE WILLING TO SETTLE FOR

Marion was struggling with whether or not she should ask that the river be clean enough for swimming. The river was so polluted, it might seem like a ludicrous goal, one that could undermine her credibility. But at the same time she wanted swimming. She would write in swimming, then cross it off, write it in, cross it off. Lieutenant Governor Richardson was sitting next to her at a rally, saw her dilemma, leaned over, and whispered in her ear, *"Ask for swimming. If you don't, you'll never get it."*

INVOLVE THE MEDIA TO GET THE WORD OUT

With that in mind, she campaigned hard. Surrounded by state legislators, she presented a jar of dirty river water to Governor Volpe at the State House. She took Senator Kennedy on a boat tour of the river, cementing his support. All this was front-page news, ideal for getting her message out.

SHARE INFORMATION

Eventually, Marion's efforts paid off. Her advocacy resulted in building a citizen coalition that collaborated with state and local government to define high water quality standards. They worked to pass the first-in-the-nation state clean water act, which paved the way for a clean Nashua River and served as a model project for other communities nationwide.

THE WORK WILL NEVER BE DONE

Of course, the Massachusetts Clean Water Act was only a start. Communities needed to build wastewater treatment plants to actually clean up the river—and though much of the bill was being footed by the federal government, cities such as Fitchburg had to put up as much as $30 million up-front, a huge sum for struggling factory towns. Marion, teaming up with Mayor Bill Flynn, was relentless in pushing for the funding and ensuring that communities followed through on their obligations. Despite the roadblocks—citizens at one point had to threaten a lawsuit against the state—the plants all came online. *"It was like a miracle,"* **Marion recalls. The water almost immediately returned to a sparkling clear.**

Restoring the Nashua isn't finished. In fact, Marion will never say that the work is done. Her evolving vision for the future is always changing to accommodate new circumstances and new goals. Although the Nashua, along with many other heavily polluted rivers, underwent an enormous transformation, there's still the invisible problem of runoff and other trace chemicals that impact the ecosystem.

As Marion's story proves, one person can make an extraordinary difference. Marion's legacy as the central advocate for the Nashua's restoration continues today with the Nashua River Watershed Association, the not-for-profit launched by Marion and her core group in 1969. Yet Marion does not see herself as an extraordinary person. Her greatest successes can be attributed to her most human qualities—her faithfulness to an outstanding vision, her longing for meaning and purpose, and her generous spirit.

As we begin to see ourselves in Marion's shoes, we can envision changes on the horizon in our own time, and feel empowered to take them on ourselves. Using this handbook and following the same steps that Marion followed, **each of us can do the work of 1000.**

"At MassInnovation, we practice sustainable development and seek to transform and revitalize our Gateway Cities. But the work can be hard and there are moments when I question whether perhaps we have bitten off more than we can chew. Fortunately for me, I'll never forget the multi-colored, polluted Nashua River I grew up with in Fitchburg and the Herculean impact a single, determined person had in cleaning it up. On more than one occasion, it was Marion Stoddart's example that helped me stay on course when it seemed like it was me against the world. For me, Marion's greatest legacy is the knowledge that with passion and perseverance, each of us can not only make a real difference in our communities, but we can also single-handedly change our world."

—ROBERT D. ANSIN
President/CEO and Founder of MassInnovation

"What I will tell you is applicable to anyone's efforts to restore a river or some other natural resource. It starts with a dream, a vision of what you want. My vision was of a restored and beautiful Nashua River teeming with fish and waterfowl and bordered by woods, meadows and other natural vegetation.

The greenway would provide natural flood storage and a buffer from pollution. It would be a continuous corridor on both sides of the river for wildlife movement and recreational trails.

Together—the river, with its protective green way, would provide a place where people could come to enjoy fishing, swimming and canoeing, or just relaxing. A river that people would enjoy being next to: to walk, bird watch, cross-country ski and horseback ride."

—MARION STODDART

START WITH A DREAM OR A VISION
OF WHAT YOU WANT

Take a few moments and imagine, really imagine—in full detail—your accomplished vision. What do you notice? What are the sights? The sounds? Who is there? What is it like for you to be there? Once you have fully explored this vision in as much detail as possible, take some time to record all that you noticed. Let all of the details pour out of you. Then let the vision inform you. Keep a lookout for ideas generated as a result. Revisit this vision whenever you want to feel connected to it.

Q: WHAT IS YOUR VISION?

A: _____

_____

_____

_____

_____

_____

_____

_____

_____

_____

_____

_____

_____

_____

Q: WHAT WILL BE DIFFERENT WHEN
   YOUR VISION IS REALIZED?

A: _____

_____

_____

_____

_____

_____

_____

_____

_____

_____

_____

_____

_____

Q: WHAT WILL IT FEEL LIKE WHEN YOU HAVE
ACCOMPLISHED YOUR VISION?

A: _____

_____

_____

_____

_____

_____

_____

_____

_____

_____

_____

_____

_____

_____

"The next step is commitment, and commitment for the long haul. You must be persistent. I made a commitment to myself to restore the Nashua River. I didn't know how long it was going to take or how I was going to do it. I thought it could take my whole lifetime."

"What I wanted to do was to make a difference in the world—which is what we all want to do—and can do. The secret to making a difference is caring and passion—it is in the degree of caring. Discovering for ourselves what matters most—creating a vision of what we want."

"You do not have to be super smart or super anything, only well informed and committed."

—MARION STODDART

COMMIT
TO THAT VISION

When you commit to something you may encounter fear.
Fear of failing, fear of success, fear of the unknown . . .
By acknowledging these fears you can become empowered
to overcome them by using your own unique gifts and talents.
Your passion. Your will. Your vision. The more you know about
yourself, the more you can bring to your vision. Check in with
yourself regularly. Asking yourself the questions: *"What am
I afraid of?"* and *"What am I really good at?"*

Q: HOW COMMITTED ARE YOU TO YOUR VISION?

A: _____

_____

_____

_____

_____

_____

_____

_____

_____

_____

_____

_____

_____

_____

_____

_____

_____

Q: WHAT DO YOU NEED TO DO IN ORDER TO
COMMIT **100%** TO YOUR VISION?

A: _____

_____

_____

_____

_____

_____

_____

_____

_____

_____

_____

_____

Q: WHAT DO YOU NEED TO LET GO OF IN
ORDER TO COMMIT **100%** TO YOUR VISION?

A: _____

_____

_____

_____

_____

_____

_____

_____

_____

_____

_____

_____

"Informing oneself and others is critical to success."

"In my own case, I spent a great deal of my time in the early 1960s learning all that I could about local, state, interstate and Federal laws regarding land and water resources and agencies that were set up to administer them. My only training came through the League of Women Voters."

–MARION STODDART

EDUCATE
YOURSELF ON THE ISSUES

Q: WHAT ARE THE SPECIFIC ISSUES YOU
   NEED TO LEARN ABOUT?

A: _____

_____

_____

_____

_____

_____

_____

_____

_____

_____

_____

_____

_____

_____

_____

_____

_____

_____

_____

_____

_____

_____

Q: WHAT RESOURCES CAN YOU USE TO
   LEARN ABOUT THESE ISSUES?

A: _____

_____

_____

_____

_____

_____

_____

_____

_____

_____

_____

_____

_____

Q: WHO ALREADY KNOWS WHAT YOU
NEED TO KNOW?

A: _____

_____

_____

_____

_____

_____

_____

_____

_____

_____

_____

_____

"I can't emphasize enough the importance of citizens' involvement. People make a difference! One person can do the work of a thousand! But strength lies in numbers. The more informed people are, the greater the power for change."

"Let people know the importance of their voice being heard. We can choose to make things better."

–MARION STODDART

EDUCATE
OTHERS

Q: WHAT DO PEOPLE NEED TO LEARN?

A: _____

_____

_____

_____

_____

_____

_____

_____

_____

_____

_____

_____

_____

_____

_____

_____

_____

_____

_____

_____

_____

_____

Q: WHO DO YOU NEED TO EDUCATE FIRST?
WHO ARE THE LEADERS AND STAKEHOLDERS?

A: _____

_____

_____

_____

_____

_____

_____

_____

_____

_____

_____

_____

_____

Q: WHEN / WHERE / HOW WILL YOU SHARE
YOUR VISION AND KNOWLEDGE WITH THEM?

A: _____

_____

_____

_____

_____

_____

_____

_____

_____

_____

_____

_____

"I was pretty well informed about the issues. I spent time identifying leaders in Massachusetts and New Hampshire communities along the river. I shared the information that I gathered and enlisted the stakeholders and leaders in my vision for the river."

"We had mayors and selectmen of all of the cities and towns along the river . . ."

—MARION STODDART

IDENTIFY COMMUNITY LEADERS AND STAKEHOLDERS

ENLIST THEM IN YOUR VISION

Broaden your perspective and look for allies by asking yourself: *"Who are the credible and respected leaders in business, government, cultural groups, educational organizations, in media, youth services, religious groups, senior centers . . . ?"* Be open to all possibilities! Friends can be found in the most unlikely places.

Q: WHAT PEOPLE OR GROUPS WILL BE AFFECTED BY OR CAN AFFECT YOUR VISION— THE STAKEHOLDERS?

A: _____

_____

_____

_____

_____

_____

_____

_____

_____

_____

_____

_____

_____

_____

_____

Q: WHO ARE THE CREDIBLE AND RESPECTED
LEADERS OF THESE GROUPS?

A: _____

_____

_____

_____

_____

_____

_____

_____

_____

_____

_____

_____

_____

Q: HOW ARE YOU ALREADY CONNECTED
TO THEM?

A: _____

_____

_____

_____

_____

_____

_____

_____

_____

_____

_____

_____

"The community leaders bring others on board and over time, we had a diverse group of thousands."

"The more people you can enlist and educate the more momentum you will gather."

"Synergy develops and it is exciting and invigorating to work together."

–MARION STODDART

BUILD
RELATIONSHIPS

Connect with your audience by speaking to them in a context they relate to and understand. Different groups may have different levels of understanding or focus that you can take into account. You may need different messages for different audiences to ensure that your message is clearly understood.

Q: WHAT WOULD YOU LIKE HELP WITH?

A: _____

_____

_____

_____

_____

_____

_____

_____

_____

_____

_____

_____

_____

_____

Q: WHO CAN HELP YOU?

A: _____

_____

_____

_____

_____

_____

_____

_____

_____

_____

_____

_____

_____

_____

Q: WHAT NEEDS TO BE IN PLACE FOR YOU
   TO ASK FOR THAT HELP?

A: _____

_____

_____

_____

_____

_____

_____

_____

_____

_____

_____

_____

_____

"Timing is everything. Most action, unfortunately, takes place only when things reach a critical stage; the Nashua was in its death throes. Importantly, we had identified all of the local and state leaders and won them to our side. It was the right time. We also enlisted the press and were getting front page coverage. It was the right time."

—MARION STODDART

INVOLVE THE MEDIA TO GET THE WORD OUT

Q: WHAT PART OF YOUR VISION WILL THE
MEDIA BE INTERESTED IN?

A: _____

_____

_____

_____

_____

_____

_____

_____

_____

_____

_____

_____

_____

_____

_____

_____
_____
_____
_____
_____
_____

Q: WHO ARE YOUR IDEAL MEDIA ALLIES?

A: _____
_____
_____
_____
_____
_____
_____
_____
_____

_____

_____

_____

_____

Q: WHAT IS YOUR "PLAN OF ACTION" TO
ENGAGE THE MEDIA IN YOUR VISION?

A: _____

_____

_____

_____

_____

_____

_____

_____

_____

_____

_____

_____

_____

"You must also be optimistic and positive thinking. Never associate with negative thinking people. You cannot change their minds. They will only draw away your energy. Only surround yourself with positive thinking people. It is exciting, synergistic, powerful, and fun."

–MARION STODDART

SURROUND
YOURSELF WITH POSITIVE
THINKING PEOPLE

Q: WHO BELIEVES IN YOUR VISION?

A: _____

_____

_____

_____

_____

_____

_____

_____

_____

_____

_____

_____

_____

_____

_____

_____

_____

_____

_____

_____

_____

_____

Q: WHO ARE YOUR VERY BEST ALLIES?

A: _____

_____

_____

_____

_____

_____

_____

_____

_____

_____

_____

_____

_____

_____

Q: WHO KEEPS YOU "CHARGED UP"
   AND EXCITED ABOUT YOUR VISION?

A: _____

_____

_____

_____

_____

_____

_____

_____

_____

_____

_____

_____

_____

"For most people, it didn't look like it was possible to restore the Nashua River and no one wants to associate themselves with a task or a challenge that they feel is impossible to reach. So we had to inspire people to believe that it was possible and that we could, by joining forces, make this happen."

"People used to say to me, 'Don't you get discouraged when people say 'no' to you?' And I would say 'no, it energizes me. It causes me to look for other doors to open to get things done. So it was always an exciting challenge.'"

—MARION STODDART

SEE "CHALLENGES" AS OPPORTUNITIES, NOT PROBLEMS

SEE "NO" AS AN EXCITING CHALLENGE

Q: WHAT OPPORTUNITIES DO YOU SEE?

A: _____

_____

_____

_____

_____

_____

_____

_____

_____

_____

_____

_____

_____

_____

_____

_____

_____

_____

_____

_____

_____

Q: HOW CAN YOU REFRAME PROBLEMS
   AS OPPORTUNITIES?

A: _____

_____

_____

_____

_____

_____

_____

_____

_____

_____

_____

_____

_____

Q: WHAT COMPROMISE(S) WILL PROVIDE
   MOMENTUM / BRING YOU CLOSER
   TO YOUR VISION?

A: _____

_____

_____

_____

_____

_____

_____

_____

_____

_____

_____

_____

". . . we spent the next year getting ready for the public hearing that was to be held to classify the river for its future highest use. We identified and personally contacted every service, social, fraternal, recreational, and conservation organization and their leaders in every town along the river. We contacted every chairman of every board of selectmen, planning board, conservation commission, board of health, recreation commission and asked them to attend the hearing too, to say how clean they wanted the river to be and why. We convinced them all that what they had to say would make a difference."

—MARION STODDART

SHARE
INFORMATION

Q: WHAT IS THE MOST IMPORTANT
   THING PEOPLE NEED TO KNOW?

A: _____

_____

_____

_____

_____

_____

_____

_____

_____

_____

_____

_____

_____

_____

_____

_____

_____

_____

_____

_____

_____

Q: WHAT IS THE MOST EFFECTIVE WAY TO SHARE THAT MESSAGE?

A: _____

_____

_____

_____

_____

_____

_____

_____

_____

_____

_____

_____

_____

Q: WHO CAN HELP YOU DELIVER
THAT MESSAGE?

A: _____

_____

_____

_____

_____

_____

_____

_____

_____

_____

_____

_____

_____

"And another early leader, which was wonderful, was the person who was in charge of the largest paper company on the river. This was Don Crocker and he said 'I'm tired of wearing a black hat, I want to wear a white hat.'"

"And Don made the first gift from his paper company and asked other companies to make a gift too. He said, 'We're all going to benefit from the cleanup of the river.'"

—MARION STODDART

BE RECEPTIVE AND OPEN TO OPPORTUNITIES FROM UNEXPECTED PLACES AND PEOPLE

Q: WHO (AND WHAT) DO YOU NOTICE
   "SHOWING UP?"

A: _____

_____

_____

_____

_____

_____

_____

_____

_____

_____

_____

_____

_____

_____

_____

_____

_____

_____

_____

_____

Q: WHAT ACTION FEELS COMPELLING?

A: _____

_____

_____

_____

_____

_____

_____

_____

_____

_____

_____

_____

Q: WHO CAN PROVIDE YOU WITH
A FRESH PERSPECTIVE?

A: _____

_____

_____

_____

_____

_____

_____

_____

_____

_____

_____

_____

_____

_____

"Something very important happened in my life September, 1967. At the airport when we were all gathered on this little podium waiting to speak, I was making my notes about what I was going to say. I would write down that we wanted fishing and swimming, boating and irrigation. Then I would cross off swimming because the Nashua River then was in such terrible condition and I wanted to be credible. They'd all seen it from the air flying into the airport so they knew how bad it was. We had recently presented a bottle of polluted Nashua River water to Governor Volpe at the State House so he knew how bad it was. I wanted to be plausible. And I wanted swimming but I wasn't sure it was the right thing politically to ask for. And so I'd cross it off my list and then I'd put it back on.

Lt. Gov. Richardson saw my dilemma and he leaned over my shoulder and whispered in my ear and said 'Ask for swimming—if you don't, you'll never get it.' And so that was one of the most important messages I've ever been given in my life. To ask for what you want, not what you're willing to settle for."

—MARION STODDART

See movie clip: http://www.workof1000.org/movies/sneak_preview.htm

ASK FOR WHAT YOU WANT, NOT WHAT YOU'RE WILLING TO SETTLE FOR

Q: IF YOU KNEW YOU COULD HAVE **ANYTHING**
YOU ASKED FOR . . . WHAT WOULD YOU
ASK FOR?

A: _____

_____

_____

_____

_____

_____

_____

_____

_____

_____

_____

_____

_____

_____

_____

_____

_____

_____

_____

_____

_____

Q: WHAT IS YOUR "BOLD" REQUEST?

A: _____

_____

_____

_____

_____

_____

_____

_____

_____

_____

_____

_____

_____

Q: WHAT DO YOU HAVE TO LET GO OF
   IN ORDER TO MAKE THAT REQUEST?

A: _____

_____

_____

_____

_____

_____

_____

_____

_____

_____

_____

_____

_____

_____

"We will always need watchdogs and stewards to ensure that laws are implemented, not weakened, and that new laws are passed when needed."

—MARION STODDART

THE WORK WILL NEVER BE DONE –THERE IS AN ONGOING STREAM OF PROGRESS TO BE MADE

Q: WHAT WILL MAINTAIN YOUR VISION IN THE FUTURE?

A: _____

_____

_____

_____

_____

_____

_____

_____

_____

_____

_____

_____

_____

_____

_____

_____

_____

_____

Q: HOW WILL YOU KNOW THAT YOUR VISION
    IS MAINTAINING ITS FORWARD MOMENTUM?

A: _____

_____

_____

_____

_____

_____

_____

_____

_____

_____

_____

_____

_____

_____

Q: WHAT IS YOUR VISION FOR PROPELLING
   YOUR VISION IN THE FUTURE?

A: _____

_____

_____

_____

_____

_____

_____

_____

_____

_____

_____

_____

AFTERWORD

Now that you have explored your vision in specific, concrete terms, you are ready to unleash your potential. The answers you wrote down in this book will remain a valuable resource as you set out to change your corner of the world. Revisit questions like *"What will be different when your vision is realized?"* when you are a year, two years, or ten years into your project. You will be amazed at what good you have accomplished. You will also be reminded that the work is never done.

The work that Marion Stoddart began in the 1960s continues today through the Nashua River Watershed Association, a leader in natural resource protection and environmental education. Visit **nashuariverwatershed.org** for the latest developments along the Nashua.

www.ingramcontent.com/pod-product-compliance
Lightning Source LLC
LaVergne TN
LVHW021546080426
835509LV00019B/2871